Simply Elegant and Easy Pesto

Mary El-Baz, Ph.D.

Copyright © 2007 Mary El-Baz, PhD
All rights reserved.
ISBN 1-4196-5436-5
ISBN-13: 978-1419654367

Visit www.booksurge.com to order additional copies.

—*To my family and friends who are captivated by the fascinating aroma and taste of pesto*

Also by Mary El-Baz

The Essence of Herbal and Floral Teas

Flavoring with Culinary Herbs: Tips, Recipes, and Cultivation

Easy and Healthful Mediterranean Cooking

Transform Your Core 6-Week Workbook

Building a Healthy Lifestyle: A Simple Nutrition and Fitness Approach

The information given here is designed to help you make informed decisions about your body and health. Its information, ideas, and suggestions are not intended as a substitute for professional medical advice. Before following any suggestions contained in this book, you should first consult your personal physician.
Neither the author nor the publisher shall be liable or responsible for any loss or damage allegedly arising as a consequence of your use or application of any information or suggestions in this book.

Table of Contents

INTRODUCTION 1

ORIGINS AND HISTORY OF PESTO 3

HEALTH BENEFITS OF PESTO 5
HERBS AND GREENS 5
NUTS AND SEEDS 8
GARLIC 9
HARD CHEESES 9
EXTRA-VIRGIN OLIVE OIL 9

TEXTURES OF PESTO 13
MORTAR AND PESTLE 13
FOOD PROCESSOR 13
BLENDER 13

STYLES OF PESTO 15
HERBAL OR CLASSIC 16
Classic Genovese Pesto 16
Trenette with Potatoes, Green Beans, and Pesto 17
Italian Cocktail Meatballs with Genovese Pesto Sauce 19
Basic Basil Pesto 20
Mediterranean Peppered Beef Tenderloin 20
Soupe au Pistou (Provençal Vegetable Soup) 21
Zucchini "Pasta" with Pesto 22
Jalapeño Cilantro Pesto 24
Jicama Salad Dressed with Jalapeño Cilantro Pesto 24

Basil-Cilantro Pesto *26*
Dill Pesto *26*
Salmon Fettuccine *27*
Fennel Pesto *28*
Red Pepper and Fennel Pesto Capellini *28*
Mint Pesto *29*
North African Mint Pesto Couscous *30*
Rosemary-Olive Pesto *30*
Rosemary-Olive Pesto on Focaccia *32*
Sage Pesto *32*
Grilled Chicken with Sage Pesto Sandwiches *33*

Greens *34*
Spinach Pesto *34*
Tallarin Verde *34*
Creamy Spinach Pesto Dressing *37*
Arugula Pesto *37*
Arugula Pesto Risotto *38*
Spicy Radicchio Pesto *39*
Radicchio Pesto Herb Crostini *41*
Radish Pesto *41*

Tomato/Pepper *42*
Sun-Dried Tomato Pesto *42*
Angel-Hair Pasta with Sun-Dried Tomato Pesto *44*
Roasted Red Pepper Pesto *44*
Roasted Red Pepper Pizza Wedges *47*
Pepperoncini Pesto *47*
Roast Beef and Pepperoncini Pesto Sandwiches *48*

ABOUT THE AUTHOR *51*

Introduction

Aromatic, pungent, and succulent flavor emanates from a dish made with pesto. Whether slathered on grilled meats, garlic bread, pizza, appetizers, pasta or potato salads. Pesto is a delight to the senses!

Pesto is an elegant and aromatic blending of a simple mince of basil and garlic with additional ingredients of nuts, cheese, and olive oil. From this very simplicity, many pesto variations have evolved, such as substituting the basil with a variety of greens or herbs, such as spinach or mint; using pine nuts, walnuts, or almonds; and romano cheese instead of parmesan.

Pesto, derived from Italian that refers to the pestle or "to pound or crush," is an Italian sauce composed of basil, garlic, cheese, nuts, and olive oil. It originates in the Liguria region of Northern Italy, specifically in the city of Genoa, which is known for its pesto, *pesto alla Genovese*. However, another well-known pesto variant exists hailing from Sicily, *pesto alla siciliana*, where the basil of Genovese pesto is replaced with tomato.

A slightly different version of the sauce exists in Provençe, where it is known as *pistou* from the Provençal dialect for "pounded." In contrast with the Italian pesto, pistou is generally made with olive oil, basil and lots of garlic; there are neither pine nuts nor cheese in the traditional recipe. Pistou is used in the typical *soupe au pistou*, a hearty vegetable soup with pistou flavor. The sauce did not originally contain basil; cheese and olive oil were the main constituents.

Pesto even made its way to the Americas. Genovese immigrants to Argentina in the nineteenth century brought pesto recipes with them. There is a popular Peruvian variety of a pesto, known as *tallarin verde*, meaning "green noodles," from the Italian *tagliarini*, is slightly creamier, uses spinach leaves and is served with potatoes and sirloin steak.

Pesto, usually sold in small jars, is commonly available in stores in the original green, or red with sun-dried tomatoes or red bell peppers varieties, produced by major manufacturers or under a "generic" brand. Pesto is easy to buy, but just as simple to make! And making it in your own kitchen is what this little book is all about.

This little book of Mediterranean flavors will take you on an exploration of the origins and history of pesto, the health benefits of pesto, the textures of pesto—smoothly creamy or lumpy pasty, and a sampling of styles of pesto—from the classic herbals to peppery greens.

Origins and History of Pesto

The origins of pesto are somehow uncertain; pesto may be a descendent of medieval garlic sauces or *agliate*, which were in turn descended from the ancient Romans' *garum*, a condiment made from fish steeped in salt and aromatic herbs. All these sauces were accompanied by *agresto*, the juice of unripe grapes, vinegar, orange juice or wine; they were not oily sauces, containing neither animal (butter) nor vegetable (olive oil) fats.

Some historical letters from the seventeenth century found in the archives of Genoa in the Liguria region of Italy mention a dressing called *battuto d'aglio,* meaning "battered garlic." The sauce that has made the region of Liguria famous the world over is named after its method of preparation: *pestatura* or grinding of leaves and other ingredients in the traditional marble *murtà* or mortar with a wooden *pestellu* or pestle.

The manner of adding oil, cheese, and nuts to the garlic sauce, likely originated in the east, where sauces were commonly made with pine nuts mixed with a tart cheese which acted as a binder holding the various ingredients together. When cheese was replaced by olive oil in its binding function, other, harder types of cheese could be used, such as Pecorino.

Basil was a much later addition to the recipe in which it was to become the most important ingredient. Basil has been known to all the Mediterranean people since the age of the Romans. The plant was imported to Europe from Asia Minor, and found its best habitat in Liguria and Provençe. The scientific name for basil, *Ocimum basilicum,* is derided from the Latin signifying "regal perfume," describing the plant's pungent, peppery taste. There are more than sixty varieties of basil, all of which differ somewhat in appearance and taste. While the taste of sweet basil is bright and pungent, other varieties also offer unique tastes: lemon basil, anise basil and cinnamon basil all have flavors that subtly reflect their name.

In Liguria and Genoa, the unique microclimate and the ideal soil favor the growth of a variety of basil especially balanced in terms of taste and aroma. In the past, it was very common for the Genovese families to keep a small basil plant on the balcony and for the captains on their ships during their long journeys.

The common pesto recipe as we know it today, first appeared in the mid-nineteenth century in writing in the Ratto brothers' 1865 *Cuciniera genovese*, where it was described as a "mince of garlic and basil" and used as a sauce with which "to dress all varieties of pasta." The correct method for conservation of the leaves, which were the most important ingredient but were not available at all times of year, was also specified in the recipe: in a vase or *arbanella*, covered with olive oil, "sealed with a parchment lid tied on with string."

There are now many different versions of the recipe for pesto, which often contain less garlic, supposedly to make the sauce easier on the digestion. Other existing ingredient variations include: arugula instead of or in addition to basil, black olives, lemon zest, cilantro, or mushroom. A variety of pasta is eaten with pesto include short, spiraled *troffie* and *trofiette* noodles; slender *trenette* noodles; the thin lasagna-type sheets known as "silk handkerchiefs," *mandilli de sae,* and even in flavoring Genovese minestrone soup.

Yet, this simply made sauce provides a multitude of health benefits…

Health Benefits of Pesto

The health benefits of pesto most certainly could be considered a sum of its parts. Nutrient rich herbs and greens, garlic, nuts and seeds, and olive oil all contribute their unique nutritional value. Plants provide phytochemicals and antioxidants. Phytochemicals are plant chemicals that help the body defend against cellular damage and are said to have anti-aging properties. Most greens contain polyphenolic compounds called flavonoids, which serve as antioxidants or play other important roles in maintaining the health of your body. Antioxidants are vitamins, minerals, or enzymes that work together to effectively neutralize free radicals, unstable cellular byproducts of our metabolism, which can travel through the body causing huge amounts of damage to cells. Free radicals are also created by our exposure to various environmental factors occurring in our daily, modern lives, such a pollution, smoke, excessive sunlight, and pesticides. Free radicals are thought to be major players in the build up of cholesterol in the arteries that leads to atherosclerosis and heart disease, the nerve and blood vessel damage seen in diabetes, the cloudy lenses of cataracts, the joint pain and damage seen in osteoarthritis and rheumatoid arthritis, and the wheezing and airway tightening of asthma.

Let's explore the nutrients of a few of the common ingredients in pesto…

Herbs and Greens
Herbs and greens are low in sodium, high in potassium, magnesium, folate, fiber, and health-promoting phytochemicals. Leafy greens have high nutrient density, meaning that they have a high proportion of nutrition—fiber, vitamins, minerals, and carbohydrates—for the few calories supplied. Leafy greens are available year round, fresh or frozen. A few of the common herbs used in pesto are basil, parsley, cilantro, fennel, dill, and rosemary and a few of the common greens from the *cruciferae* or mustard family, such as spinach, arugula, and radishes, are used. They are loaded with the flavonoid antioxidants that scavenge the free radicals and they are also filled with carotenoids which also act as antioxidants and as preventive agents of cancer cells; the yellow pigment of the carotenoids is covered up by the chlorophyll of the greens. The crucifers are rich in the indoles and sulforaphanes that block cancer-causing agents from reaching cells.

Starting with the herbs, basil is a very good source of iron, calcium and vitamin A. In addition, basil is a good source of dietary fiber, manganese, magnesium, vitamin C, and potassium. Research studies on basil have shown unique health-protecting effects in two basic areas: basil's flavonoids and volatile oils. Its flavonoids provide protection at the cellular level, while its volatile oils have been shown to have anti-bacterial properties.

Parsley, cilantro, dill, and fennel are members of the *umbelliferous* group of plants and are extremely rich sources of phytochemicals. Parsley is a native of the Mediterranean region of Europe and has been cultivated for over two thousand years as a medicinal plant. Parsley is an excellent source of vitamins A, C, and K, and folate. It is a very good source of iron and a good source of vitamin E and dietary fiber as well as a host of minerals including potassium, calcium, magnesium, and manganese.

Cilantro is rich in beneficial phytonutrients, flavonoids and active phenolic acid compounds. Cilantro and its seeds, known as coriander, have been found to help control blood sugar, lower cholesterol and fight inflammation and free radicals. Cilantro may also have antimicrobial properties.

Dill's unique health benefits come from flavonoids and phenols, another strong antioxidant from plants. It is a good source of calcium, dietary fiber, and the minerals manganese, iron, and magnesium.

Fennel is an excellent source of vitamin C. It is also a very good source of dietary fiber, potassium, manganese, folate, and molybdenum. In addition, fennel is a good source of niacin as well as the minerals phosphorous, calcium, magnesium, iron, and copper. Like many of its fellow spices, fennel contains its own unique combination of phytonutrients.

The wonderful smell of rosemary is often associated with good food. Rosemary contains several different phytochemicals that studies have shown to be antioxidant, anti-inflammatory, and antibacterial. It is a good source of the minerals iron and calcium, as well as dietary fiber.

Moving on to the leafy greens, spinach is a super source of antioxidants and cancer preventive agents. It is an excellent source of vitamins A, B2, B6, C, and K; manganese; folate; magnesium; iron; calcium; and potassium. It is a very good source of dietary fiber, copper, protein, phosphorous, zinc, and vitamin E. In addition, it is a good source of omega-3 fatty acids, niacin, and selenium.

Arugula, also called rocket or rucola, is a deep green vegetable with long, slender leaves that is widely used in Italian cooking. It is peppery and aromatic, with a pungent, somewhat bitter flavor. Arugula looks like a kind of lettuce, but it is a cruciferous vegetable and has many of the same potent health benefits of this group. Arugula is rich in phytonutrients and vitamins A and C.

The radish is thought to be native to Asia, but domesticated in the Mediterranean. The radish is another member of the mustard family and like other members of this family; radishes contain sulphurous compounds that have anti-cancer properties. Radishes provide vitamin C, potassium, magnesium, iron, sulphur, folate, and amylase to help with digestion of carbohydrates.

The tomato, though not a "green," is a major source of lycopene, an antioxidant and anti-cancer agent that neutralizes free radicals. Tomatoes are an excellent source of vitamins A and C. They are also a very good source of vitamins B1 and K, molybdenum, potassium, manganese, dietary fiber, and chromium. In addition, tomatoes are a good source of vitamins B2, B6, and E; folate; copper; niacin; magnesium; iron; pantothenic acid; phosphorous; and protein.

The bell pepper is an excellent source of vitamins A and C, along with a concentration of carotenoids such as beta-carotene. Red bell peppers are also an excellent source of the vitamins K and B6. In addition to beta-carotene, red bell peppers contain the beneficial phytonutrients lycopene, lutein, and zeaxanthin. Green bell peppers are a very good source of fiber and folate as well as the minerals molybdenum and manganese.

Nuts and Seeds

Nuts and seeds are rich in protein, fiber, vitamins, and minerals. These supernutritives are a top source of antioxidant phytochemicals such as lignans, monoterpenes, and polyphenols. They are rich in high amounts of all the B-complex vitamins, vitamin E, iron, magnesium, potassium, phosphorous, zinc, copper, and selenium. Nuts and seeds have high amounts of essential fatty acids and contain liberal amounts of omega-6 with some omega-3 fatty acids. These are the "good" fats that help regulate blood cholesterol levels and keep our tissues and skin supple. Walnuts and almonds help reduce cholesterol, contain high concentrations of antioxidant oleic acid and monounsaturated fat, similar to that in olive oil. Walnuts also contain ellagic acid, an antioxidant and cancer preventive agent, and are also high in omega-3 type oil. Nuts are good regulators of insulin and blood sugar, preventing steep rises, making them good foods for those with glucose intolerance and diabetes.

Pine nuts, also called Indian nut, piñon, pignoli, and pignolia, come from several varieties of pine trees. The nuts are actually inside the pine cone, which generally must be heated to facilitate their removal. Pine nuts grow in China, Italy, Mexico, North Africa, and the southwestern United

States. When raw, the seeds have a soft texture and a sweet, buttery flavor. They are often lightly toasted to bring out the flavor and to add a little crunch.

Garlic

The distinctive fragrance of garlic is the result of the sulfur-containing compounds that also provide many of its health benefits. Garlic contains multiple anti-cancer compounds and antioxidants and is included on the National Cancer Institute's list as a potential cancer-preventive food. Garlic is an excellent source of manganese, and provides plenty of vitamin B6 and vitamin C. Calcium selenium, phosphorus, copper, and protein are also available in this pungent vegetable.

Studies show that regular consumption of garlic lowers blood pressure and harmful low-density lipoproteins (LDL) cholesterol levels. The vitamin B6 in garlic appears helps to reduce heart-damaging homocysteine levels.

Hard Cheeses

The typical cheeses used in pesto are the Parmesan-type cheeses, such as Parmesan and Romano, however aged Asiago or *asiago d'allevo,* whose flavor is reminiscent of sharp Parmesan, can be used. Parmesan's taste is delicate, fragrant and very savory compared to the sharper and more piquant flavor of Romano. The taste of Parmesan intensifies with age. Parmesan originated in the Reggio and Parma regions of Italy, and Parmesan from these regions is known by more specific names such as "Parmigiano-Reggiano," a rich and creamy cheese or "Pecorino-Romano," which has a sharper flavor. The original Parmagiano-Reggiano reflects over eight hundred years of tradition and is considered one of the great cheeses of the world. All Parmesan cheese produced outside these two regions in Italy is known simply as Parmesan.

Cheese is a natural food providing a dense source of nutrients. It is a good source of calcium and protein. Calcium is essential for growing and maintaining strength and density of bones and teeth, and preventing osteoporosis. It supports normal cardiovascular, thyroid, and muscular function.

Extra-Virgin Olive Oil

Olive oil is a natural juice which preserves the taste, aroma, vitamins and properties of the olive fruit. Olive oil is the only vegetable oil that can be consumed freshly pressed from the fruit. However, while all types of olive oil are sources of monounsaturated fat, extra-virgin olive oil, from the first pressing of the olives, contains higher levels of antioxidants, particularly vitamin E and phenols, because it is less processed. Olive oil does not upset our body's critical omega-6 to omega-3 essential fatty acid ratio and most of the fatty acids in olive oil are actually omega-9, which is monounsaturated. Olive oil is very well tolerated by the stomach. In fact, olive oil's protective function has a beneficial effect on ulcers and gastritis.

The beneficial health effects of olive oil are due to both its high content of monounsaturated fatty acids and its high content of antioxidative substances. Studies have shown that olive oil offers protection against heart disease by controlling LDL, the "bad," cholesterol levels while raising high-density lipoproteins (HDL), the "good," cholesterol levels.

Now, let's see how to get those different textures of pesto sauce….

Textures of Pesto

Mortar and Pestle

The ancient method of preparation of pesto is with a marble mortar and a wooden pestle. This traditional method is still considered to be the best way of preparing pesto at home, although in today's fast-paced world, very few cooks actually follow this process. The crushing of the leaves produces a smooth and aromatic paste creating an impressive melding of flavors.

In order to allow the full release of basil leaf aroma, the leaves should be squeezed by using a crushing motion of the turning of the wrist while holding the pestle against the mortar. This squeezing, crushing action brings out the fine, delicate, aromatic fragrance of the herbs. The movement of the wrist is of great importance. It should be a round movement, allowing a squeezing action, rather than a pounding action. Additionally, the heavier the pestle, the faster the work. Once the leaves have been squeezed, some extra-virgin olive oil is poured in, along with salt and this mixture is squeezed again. At the end, the parmesan cheese and the pine nuts, and a bit more olive oil, are added in. The result should be a creamy pesto, thick but not hard solid.

The mortars tend to be better than food processors or blenders for working with a small volume of ingredients.

Food Processor

Squeezing, crushing, or pounding the leaves in a mortar is somewhat tedious and time-consuming for today's cooks, so often a food processor is used to save the time and effort of working with a pestle. The food processor produces a satisfactory paste, although the ingredients are not as integrated as that with the mortar and pestle. Each ingredient retains a bit of its original identity, the action of the blades not able to bring about the unique fragrant compounds brought about by the mortar and pestle method.

Blender

Using a blender rather than a food processor makes a smoother purée creating a sauce texture. It should have the consistency of a thick sauce. The food processor tends not to purée the basil enough nor emulsify the oil enough to make it into a smooth thickness, so liquid may be added to ensure the smoothness. Finely dice the herbs, garlic, and nuts before placing them into the blender. Prepare this way when you want more of a dipping, drizzling type of sauce, as with Asian or Mexican dishes.

Styles of Pesto

The styles of pesto are so varied! A variety of herbs and greens, nuts and seeds, and cheeses can be used. Pesto is a delicious enhancement to grilled meats, garlic bread, pizza, appetizers, salads, and, of course, a variety of pastas.

The recipes in this chapter are classified into three categories: Herbal or Classic, Greens, and Tomato/Pepper. You'll find the basic basil pesto as well as some zesty cilantro, cool dill, and fennel pesto recipes in the Herbal or Classic section. The piquant and unexpected flavors of arugula and radicchio can be found in the pesto recipes in the Greens section. And the sunny, coastal Mediterranean flavors of sun-dried tomatoes and roasted red peppers appear in the pesto recipes in the Tomato/Pepper section. All can be prepared in the traditional, food processor, or blender manner, yet most of the recipes use the food processor method.

Whichever method you choose to prepare your pesto, be it the traditional manner with mortar and pestle, food processor, or blender, all are sure to please your eye, nose, and palate!

Here are helpful tips to keep in mind while you are preparing your pesto:
- When storing basil pesto in the fridge, cover the top of it with a thin layer of olive oil to prevent it from turning brown
- Add basil pesto into or onto heated foods right before serving, as that it browns quickly when heated
- Always remove the stems from basil, using only the leaves, because the stems will darken pesto's classic brilliant bright green color
- Portion amounts made from each pesto recipe are approximate and may vary among the different preparation methods: traditional, food processor, or blender
- Use more or less pesto than that stated in the recipe according to your taste

Herbal or Classic

Classic Genovese Pesto
Prepared in the traditional manner with mortar and pestle

1 large bunch of fresh basil leaves
4 cloves garlic, peeled
1 teaspoon pine nuts
5 to 6 tablespoons Ligurian extra-virgin olive oil
¾ cup freshly grated Pecorino-Romano cheese

1. Do not wash the basil. Simply wipe the leaves carefully with paper towels or a clean cloth to remove any dirt. Remove and discard the stems.
2. Place a few leaves of basil in a medium-sized mortar.
3. Add a clove of garlic and squeeze-crush the leaves and garlic against the sides of the mortar using the pestle.
4. Add a few more leaves of basil and another garlic clove, and repeat the process.
5. Once all the basil and garlic have been crushed, add the pine nuts. Crush until the basil, garlic, and pine nuts are well blended.
6. Add a tablespoon of olive oil and combine with the ingredients in the mortar. Then add the Pecorino-Romano a little at a time, stirring with a wooden spoon. Then stir in some more oil, a tablespoon at a time, until a a thick, creamy sauce results. It is not necessary to use all of the oil.

Makes about ½ cup

Simply Elegant and Easy Pesto

Trenette with Potatoes, Green Beans, and Pesto

This is a typical Genoese pasta using the classic Ligurian pasta trenette or noodles. Some cooks add a bit of hot water from the pasta pot to dilute the pesto just before it is tossed with the noodles.

8 ounces packaged Ligurian trenette (slender noodles with a ribbed edge) pasta or linguine
1 tablespoon extra-virgin olive oil
3 medium boiling or red potatoes, peeled and thinly sliced
1 cup fresh green beans or haricots, blanched
½ cup Classic Genovese Pesto

1. In a large saucepan, add 3 quarts of water and bring to boiling. Add 1 tablespoon olive oil to keep the pasta separated.
2. Add the pasta a little at a time so the water does not stop boiling. Add the potatoes. Reduce heat slightly and boil, uncovered. Stir occasionally.
3. Cook about 7 to 8 minutes or until pasta and potatoes are cooked through. Drain pasta and potatoes at once.
4. Transfer to a warm platter and toss with the green beans and pesto. Serve very hot, accompanied by a bowl of grated Pecorino cheese.

Serves 6 to 8

Simply Elegant and Easy Pesto

Italian Cocktail Meatballs with Genovese Pesto Sauce

1 beaten egg
¼ cup fine dry bread crumbs, Italian style
¼ cup tomato juice
2 tablespoons fresh snipped parsley
1 teaspoon dry mustard
⅛ teaspoon salt
Dash pepper
1 pound lean ground beef or turkey
1 tablespoon butter
1 tablespoon all-purpose flour
Dash pepper
¾ cup low-fat milk
¼ cup Genovese Pesto
Finely crumbled Pecorino-Romano cheese

Preheat oven to 350° F.

Prepare meatballs:

1. In a bowl, combine egg, bread crumbs, tomato juice, parsley, mustard, salt, and pepper. Add beef or turkey. Mix well.
2. Shape into 1-inch meatballs. Place in a 15 x 10 x 1-inch baking pan. Bake in 350° F oven for 15 to 18 minutes or till done. Drain.

Prepare Genovese Pesto Sauce:

1. In a medium saucepan, melt butter.
2. Stir in flour and pepper. Add milk all at once.
3. Cook and stir over medium-low until thickened and bubbly.
4. Add the pesto and Pecorino-Romano cheese crumbles, and stir gently to combine.

Add meatballs to the pesto sauce; gently turn with spoon to mix and coat; heat thorough. Spoon onto a serving dish.

Makes about 10 servings

Basic Basil Pesto

¼ cup pine nuts or walnuts or almonds
2 large cloves garlic
1 cup packed fresh basil leaves
½ cup packed fresh parsley leaves, stems removed
½ cup grated Parmesan or Romano cheese
⅛ teaspoon salt
¼ cup extra-virgin olive oil

1. Put nuts and garlic in a food processor and process until minced.
2. Add basil, parsley, cheese, and salt and process until finely minced.
3. With processor on, slowly pour oil through food chute; process until well blended.
4. Spoon into small container and store in the refrigerator. Or freeze portion up to 1 month.

Makes about ¾ cup

Mediterranean Peppered Beef Tenderloin

4 6- to 7-ounce beef tenderloin steaks
1 tablespoon garlic, minced
1/2 teaspoon salt
4 tablespoons coarse ground peppercorn medley (red, green, black peppercorn mixture)
2 tablespoons extra-virgin olive oil
4 tablespoons Basic Basil Pesto

Simply Elegant and Easy Pesto

Preheat oven to 350° F.

1. Rinse and dry the steaks. Rub each steak with garlic and salt. Sprinkle 1 tablespoon peppercorns over each steak.
2. In a large skillet, heat the olive oil. Place the steaks in the preheated pan, peppercorn side down first, and cook for 3 to 4 minutes.
3. Flip steaks over and cook an additional 3 to 4 minutes for medium rare.
4. To cook steaks more, finish in a preheated 350° F until the steak has reached desired doneness.
5. Spoon about 1 tablespoon pesto over the top of each steak.

Serves 4

Soupe au Pistou (Provençal Vegetable Soup)

2 cans (19-ounces) cannellini beans, drained and rinsed
¼ cup olive oil
4 garlic cloves, peeled and minced
4 small leeks, cleaned, trimmed, and minced
4 carrots, diced
2 celery ribs with leaves, sliced into ½-inch pieces
2 potatoes, peeled and cut into ½-inch cubes
12 cups water
1 14.5-ounce can diced tomatoes
½ pound fresh green beans, cut into 1-inch pieces
1 small zucchini, seeded, and cut into ½-inch cubes
4 ounces orzo pasta
Salt and pepper to taste
¾ cup Basic Basil Pesto

1. In a large pot over medium-high heat, heat olive oil and add the garlic, leeks, carrots, and celery and sauté 5 to 7 minutes.

2. Add the potatoes. Cover the vegetables with the water and stir in the tomatoes. Season with salt and pepper. Bring to a boil, and simmer, uncovered, 40 to 45 minutes.
3. Add the cannellini beans, green beans, zucchini, and pasta and continue simmering until the vegetables are tender and the pasta is cooked, about 15 to 20 minutes.
4. Ladle the soup into bowls and stir in 2 to 3 teaspoons of the pesto (pistou). The extra pistou should be passed at the table so that more can be added if desired.

Serves 10 to 12

Zucchini "Pasta" with Pesto

The unexpected, the pasta is zucchini!

1 tablespoon pine nuts
3 medium zucchini, peeled and ends cut off
2 medium roma tomatoes, seeded and chopped
1 tablespoon extra-virgin olive oil
Salt and black pepper to taste
4 basil leaves for garnish
½ cup Basic Basil Pesto
Spiral vegetable slicer or mandoline

1. Toast pine nuts in a small heavy pan over medium heat, stirring occasionally, until lightly golden, 3 to 4 minutes. Transfer nuts to a plate and let cool.
2. Using a spiral vegetable slicer or mandoline, slice the zucchini into spiral "noodles" or thin julienne strips, discarding any seeds. Place the zucchini noodles in a medium bowl and add chopped tomatoes, and olive oil. Season with salt and black pepper, if desired.
3. Gently toss the zucchini and tomato mixture with just enough pesto to coat.
4. Garnish zucchini "pasta" with the toasted pine nuts and basil leaves as garnish.

Serves 4

Jalapeño Cilantro Pesto

1 small jalapeño pepper, stemmed, seeded, and chopped
2 cups packed fresh cilantro leaves, stems removed
½ cup packed fresh parsley leaves, stems removed
1 medium clove garlic
¼ cup grated Asiago cheese
⅛ teaspoon salt
¼ cup extra-virgin olive oil
¼ cup water

1. Pour enough of the oil in a blender to cover the blade. Add in the pepper, cilantro, parsley, garlic, cheese, salt, and the rest of the oil.
2. Purée until the pesto is thick and smooth, adding water as needed.
3. Spoon into small container and store in the refrigerator. Or freeze portions up to 1 month.

Makes about ½ to ¾ cup

Jicama Salad Dressed with Jalapeño Cilantro Pesto

1 Jicama, peeled and julienned
1 yellow bell pepper, seeded and julienned
1 red bell pepper, seeded and julienned
1 ripe avocado, chopped, dressed with 1 tablespoon lemon juice
½ cup Jalapeño Cilantro Pesto

1. In a large bowl, combine jicama and peppers with the Jalapeño Cilantro Pesto, toss, and refrigerate. Chill up to 4 hours.
2. When ready to serve, put dressed julienned jicama and bell peppers on a salad plate and top with the chunks of avocado.

Serves 8

Basil-Cilantro Pesto

¼ cup pine nuts or walnuts or almonds
2 large cloves garlic
1 cup packed fresh basil leaves
½ cup packed fresh cilantro leaves, stems removed
½ cup grated Parmesan or Romano cheese
⅛ teaspoon salt
¼ cup extra-virgin olive oil

1. Put nuts and garlic in a food processor and process until minced.
2. Add basil, cilantro, cheese, and salt and process until finely minced.
3. With processor on, slowly pour oil through food chute; process until well blended.
4. Spoon into small container and store in the refrigerator. Or freeze portion up to 1 month.

Makes about ¾ cup

Dill Pesto

¼ cup pine nuts or walnuts
1 large clove garlic
Lemon zest from 1 small lemon
1 cup packed fresh dill leaves, stems removed
¼ cup packed fresh parsley leaves, stems removed
¼ cup grated Romano cheese
⅛ teaspoon salt
¼ cup extra-virgin olive oil

1. Put nuts and garlic in a food processor and process until minced.
2. Add lemon zest, dill, parsley, cheese, and salt and process until finely minced.
3. With processor on, slowly pour oil through food chute; process until well blended.

4. Spoon into small container and store in the refrigerator. Or freeze portions up to 1 month.

Makes about ¾ cup

Salmon Fettuccine

8 ounces packaged fettuccine pasta
1 tablespoon extra-virgin olive oil
1 10-ounce package of frozen green peas
8 ounces fresh or frozen (thawed) salmon fillet, sliced into thin 2 x 1-inch pieces
1 tablespoon butter
1 tablespoon all-purpose flour
Dash pepper
¾ cup low-fat milk
¼ cup Dill Pesto

1. Bring a large pot of water and 1 tablespoon olive oil to a boil. Add pasta and cook, stirring often, 7 minutes. Add peas; boil 5 to 6 minutes until pasta is firm tender.
2. Meanwhile, in a medium saucepan, melt butter.
3. Stir in flour and pepper. Add milk all at once.
4. Cook and stir over medium-low until thickened and bubbly.
5. Add the salmon, and stirring gently, simmer 3 to 5 minutes until fish is tender.
6. Add the dill pesto, and stir gently to combine.
7. Remove ½ cup cooking water from pasta pot. Drain pasta and peas; return to pot.
8. Add salmon and dill sauce, and reserved cooking water. Gently turn with spoon to mix and coat.
9. Pour into a serving dish and serve.

Serves 6

Fennel Pesto

¼ cup pine nuts or walnuts
1 large clove garlic
1 cup packed fresh fennel leaves, stems removed
¼ cup packed fresh parsley leaves, stems removed
¼ cup grated Romano cheese
⅛ teaspoon salt
¼ cup extra-virgin olive oil

1. Toast nuts in a small heavy pan over medium heat, stirring occasionally, until lightly golden, 3 to 4 minutes. Transfer nuts to a plate and let cool.
2. Toast garlic clove with its skin on in a small heavy pan over medium heat until slightly brown, about 10 minutes. Transfer to a plate, cool, and peel.
3. Put toasted nuts and garlic in a food processor and process until minced.
4. Add fennel, parsley, cheese, and salt and process until finely minced.
5. With processor on, slowly pour oil through food chute; process until well blended.
6. Spoon into small container and store in the refrigerator. Or freeze portions up to 1 month.

Makes about ¾ cup

Red Pepper and Fennel Pesto Capellini

Featured on the front cover!

4 ounces capellini or angel-hair pasta
1 tablespoon extra-virgin olive oil
½ cup Fennel Pesto
Salt and black pepper to taste
½ tablespoon red pepper flakes
Thinly sliced red bell pepper for garnish

Simply Elegant and Easy Pesto

1. In a large saucepan, add 3 quarts of water and bring to boiling. Add 1 tablespoon olive oil to keep the pasta separated.
2. Add the pasta a little at a time so the water does not stop boiling. Reduce heat slightly and boil, uncovered. Stir occasionally.
3. Cook for 5 minutes. Test for doneness, pasta is tender but still firm. Drain in a colander.
4. Place the pasta in a medium bowl and season with salt and black pepper, if desired.
5. Gently toss the pasta with just enough fennel pesto to coat. Sprinkle red pepper flakes on top and garnish with the thin red bell pepper slices.

Serves 4

Mint Pesto

¼ **cup almonds**
2 large cloves garlic
1 cup packed fresh mint leaves
½ **cup packed fresh parsley leaves, stems removed**
½ **cup grated Parmesan or Romano cheese**
⅛ **teaspoon salt**
¼ **cup extra-virgin olive oil**

1. Put almonds and garlic in a food processor and process until minced.
2. Add mint, parsley, cheese, and salt and process until finely minced.
3. With processor on, slowly pour oil through food chute; process until well blended.
4. Spoon into small container and store in the refrigerator. Or freeze portion up to 1 month.

Makes about ¾ cup

North African Mint Pesto Couscous

1¼ cups water
¼ teaspoon salt
⅔ cup couscous
¼ cup Mint Pesto
1 small cucumber, peeled, seeded, and diced
Mint sprig for garnish

1. Place water and salt in a saucepan, and bring to boiling.
2. Stir in couscous. Cover; remove from heat.
3. Let stand 5 minutes. Stir in mint pesto and cucumber, toss gently to combine.
4. Place in serving dish and garnish with mint sprig, if desired.

Serves 4

Rosemary-Olive Pesto

Similar to a tapanade. An excellent appetizer spread!

¼ cup sunflower seeds
1 medium clove garlic
¼ cup packed fresh rosemary leaves
½ cup packed fresh parsley leaves, stems removed
4 ounces of finely chopped Kalamata or black olives
¼ cup grated Parmesan or Romano cheese
⅛ teaspoon salt
¼ cup extra-virgin olive oil

1. Put seeds and garlic in a food processor and process until minced.
2. Add rosemary, parsley, olives, cheese, and salt and process until finely minced.
3. With processor on, slowly pour oil through food chute; process until well blended.
4. Spoon into small container and store in the refrigerator. Or freeze portions up to 1 month.

Makes about ¾ cup

Rosemary-Olive Pesto on Focaccia

12 2-inch square slices of focaccia bread
½ cup Rosemary-Olive Pesto
Grated Parmesan cheese for garnish

1. Spread the focaccia slices evenly with Rosemary-Olive Pesto.
2. Sprinkle evenly with Parmesan cheese.

Serves 12

Sage Pesto

¼ cup walnuts
2 large cloves garlic
1 cup lightly packed fresh sage leaves, stems removed
½ cup packed fresh parsley, stems removed
½ cup grated Parmesan or Romano cheese
⅛ teaspoon salt
¼ cup extra-virgin olive oil

1. Put walnuts and garlic in a food processor and process until minced.
2. Add sage, parsley, cheese, and salt and process until finely minced.
3. With processor on, slowly pour oil through food chute; process until well blended.
4. Spoon into small container and store in the refrigerator. Or freeze portions up to 1 month.

Makes about ¾ cup

Simply Elegant and Easy Pesto

Grilled Chicken with Sage Pesto Sandwiches

4 skinless boneless chicken breast halves
3 tablespoons extra-virgin olive oil
4 4 x 5-inch rectangles focaccia, ciabatta, or long French rolls, split horizontally
Low-fat mayonnaise
2 cups shredded Romaine letture
1 thinly sliced tomato
½ cup Sage Pesto
Salt and pepper to taste
Waxed paper

1. Place each chicken breast between sheets of waxed paper. Using rolling pin or meat mallet, pound each to ½-inch thickness. Brush chicken with 3 tablespoons oil; sprinkle with salt and pepper. Let chicken stand 30 minutes.
2. Prepare grill and over medium heat, grill chicken until firm to touch and cooked through, about 5 minutes per side. Transfer chicken to platter. Grill focaccia or ciabatta bread, or French rolls until just beginning to brown, about 1 minute per side.
3. Arrange bottom halves of bread on work surface. Spread each with mayonnaise. Sprinkle with shredded Romaine lettuce and a few slices of the sliced tomato (be sure to evenly divide the lettuce and tomato into fourths). Top each with a chicken breast.
4. Spoon 1½ tablespoons of sage pesto over each chicken breast. Place bread tops on chicken. Cut sandwiches in half on diagonal. Transfer sandwiches to plates and serve.

Serves 4

Greens

Spinach Pesto

¼ cup pine nuts or walnuts or almonds
2 large cloves garlic
1 cup packed fresh spinach leaves, stems removed
½ cup packed fresh parsley leaves, stems removed
½ cup grated Parmesan or Romano cheese
⅛ teaspoon salt
¼ cup extra-virgin olive oil

1. Put nuts and garlic in a food processor and process until minced.
2. Add spinach, parsley, cheese, and salt and process until finely minced.
3. With processor on, slowly pour oil through food chute; process until well blended.
4. Spoon into small container and store in the refrigerator. Or freeze portions up to 1 month.

Makes about ¾ cup

Tallarin Verde
Peruvian "Green Noodles" and Steak

4 ounces whole wheat spaghetti
3 tablespoons extra-virgin olive oil
6 small baby Dutch potatoes, scrubbed and quartered
8 ounces thin-cut steak (strip steak)
½ cup Italian-style bread crumbs
⅛ teaspoon salt

Simply Elegant and Easy Pesto

¼ teaspoon pepper
⅛ teaspoon garlic powder
1 cup young green beans, blanched
½ cup Spinach Pesto

1. In a large saucepan, add 3 quarts of water and bring to boiling. Add 1 tablespoon olive oil to keep the pasta separated.
2. Add the pasta a little at a time so the water does not stop boiling. Add the potatoes. Reduce heat slightly and boil, uncovered. Stir occasionally.
3. Cook about 7 to 8 minutes or until pasta and potatoes are cooked through. Drain pasta and potatoes at once.
4. Place potatoes in a saucepan with 1 tablespoon extra-virgin olive oil and cook until golden brown. Remove from pan and set aside.
5. Trim fat off of steak and cut into four equal pieces. Season with salt, pepper and garlic powder. Spread bread crumbs on a flat plate and coat steak with layer of bread crumbs on both sides.
6. Heat 1 to 2 tablespoons extra-virgin olive oil in a large skillet, place the steak, and cook until golden brown.
7. Gently toss the spaghetti with the spinach pesto. Turn out onto a large serving platter.
8. Set the steak on top of the spaghetti and spoon the green beans and potatoes all around the sides of the spaghetti.

Serves 3 to 4

Simply Elegant and Easy Pesto

Creamy Spinach Pesto Dressing

¾ cup mayonnaise or salad dressing
¼ cup low-fat sour cream or plain nonfat yogurt
2 teaspoons white balsamic vinegar
¼ cup Spinach Pesto
1 to 2 tablespoons low-fat milk

1. In a mixing bowl, stir together mayonnaise or salad dressing, sour cream or yogurt, vinegar, and pesto.
2. Cover and store in the refrigerator up to 2 weeks. If necessary, stir in milk 1 tablespoon at a time to adjust consistency.

Makes 1 cup (16 1-tablespoon servings)

Arugula Pesto

¼ cup walnuts
2 large cloves garlic
1 cup packed arugula leaves
½ cup packed fresh parsley leaves, stems removed
½ cup grated Romano cheese
⅛ teaspoon salt
¼ cup extra-virgin olive oil

1. Toast walnuts in a small heavy pan over medium heat, stirring occasionally, until lightly golden, 3 to 4 minutes. Transfer nuts to a plate and let cool.
2. Toast garlic cloves with their skins on in a small heavy pan over medium heat until lightly brown in places, about 10 minutes. Transfer to a plate, let cool, and remove the skins.
3. Put toasted walnuts and garlic in a food processor and process until minced.

4. Add arugula, parsley, cheese, and salt and process until finely minced.
5. With processor on, slowly pour oil through food chute; process until well blended.
6. Spoon into small container and store in the refrigerator. Or freeze portions up to 1 month.

Makes about ¾ cup

Arugula Pesto Risotto

A great accompaniment to grilled fish or chicken!

1 tablespoon unsalted butter
1 small yellow onion, finely chopped
1 cup Arborio rice
½ cup dry white wine
2 cups low-sodium chicken broth
½ cup grated Parmesan cheese
⅛ teaspoon salt
¼ teaspoon black pepper
¼ cup Arugula Pesto

1. Melt the butter in a large saucepan over medium heat. Add the onion and cook for 3 minutes.
2. Add the rice and cook, stirring constantly, for 2 minutes. Reduce heat to medium-low.
3. Add the wine and cook, stirring frequently, until the liquid is absorbed. Add the broth, ½ cup at a time, stirring occasionally and waiting for the broth to be absorbed before adding more. All the broth should be absorbed within 30 minutes.
4. Remove from heat and stir in the cheese, salt, and pepper, then stir in the pesto.

Serves 4

Simply Elegant and Easy Pesto

Spicy Radicchio Pesto

Excellent as a mouth-watering appetizer spread on herb crostini!

¼ cup walnuts
2 large cloves garlic
1 cup firmly packed shredded radicchio leaves
½ cup lightly packed fresh parsley leaves, stems removed
¼ cup grated Parmesan cheese
⅛ teaspoon salt
¼ cup extra-virgin olive oil

1. Put walnuts and garlic in a food processor and process until minced.
2. Add radicchio, parsley, cheese, and salt and process until finely minced.
3. With processor on, slowly pour oil through food chute; process until well blended.
4. Spoon into small container and store in the refrigerator. Or freeze portions up to 1 month.

Makes about ¾ cup

Simply Elegant and Easy Pesto

Radicchio Pesto Herb Crostini

24 slices (¼- to ½-inch thick) herb or plain baguette bread
¼ cup extra-virgin olive oil
¾ cup Spicy Radicchio Pesto

Preheat oven to 400° F.

1. Arrange the bread slices on 2 heavy large baking sheets. Brush each slice with oil. Bake until pale golden and crisp, about 5 minutes.
2. Spread about 1 teaspoon pesto over each crostini. Arrange on a platter and serve.

Makes 24

Radish Pesto

An extraordinarily mild, refreshing taste! Perfect as a dressing on Asian-style salads.

¼ cup walnuts
1 large clove garlic
1 cup shredded Daikon radish
¼ cup fresh parsley leaves, stems removed
¼ cup grated Parmesan or Romano cheese
⅛ teaspoon salt
¼ cup extra-virgin olive oil

1. Put walnuts and garlic in a food processor and process until minced.
2. Add grated radish, parsley, cheese, and salt and process until finely minced.
3. With processor on, slowly pour oil through food chute; process until well blended.
4. Spoon into small container and store in the refrigerator. Or freeze portion up to 1 month.

Makes about ¾ cup

Tomato/Pepper

Sun-Dried Tomato Pesto

¼ cup walnuts
2 large cloves garlic
8 pieces of sun-dried tomatoes (about ¼ cup) packed dry (reduce olive oil by 1 tablespoon of using packed in oil), chopped
1 tablespoon fresh parsley leaves, stems removed
¼ cup grated Parmesan or Romano cheese
⅛ teaspoon salt
¼ cup extra-virgin olive oil

1. Put walnuts and garlic in a food processor and process until minced.
2. Add tomatoes, parsley, cheese, and salt and process until finely minced.
3. With processor on, slowly pour oil through food chute; process until well blended.
4. Spoon into small container and store in the refrigerator. Or freeze portion up to 1 month.

Makes about ¾ cup

Angel-Hair Pasta with Sun-Dried Tomato Pesto

4 ounces angel-hair pasta
1 tablespoon extra-virgin olive oil
½ cup Sun-Dried Tomato Pesto
Salt and pepper to taste

1. In a large saucepan, add 3 quarts of water and bring to boiling. Add 1 tablespoon olive oil to keep the pasta separated.
2. Add the pasta a little at a time so the water does not stop boiling. Reduce heat slightly and boil, uncovered. Stir occasionally.
3. Cook for 3 to 5 minutes. Test for doneness, pasta is tender but still firm. Drain in a colander.
4. Place the pasta in a medium bowl. Season with salt and black pepper, if desired.
5. Gently toss the pasta with just enough sun-dried tomato pesto to coat.

Serves 4

Roasted Red Pepper Pesto
Super with all types of pizza dishes! Roast your own red peppers or use canned roasted peppers.

2 large cloves garlic
1 cup peeled roasted red bell peppers or canned roasted red bell peppers, drained
½ cup lightly packed fresh parsley leaves, stems removed
¼ cup grated Parmesan or Romano cheese
⅛ teaspoon salt
¼ cup extra-virgin olive oil

Simply Elegant and Easy Pesto

To roast red peppers:

Preheat oven to 400° F.

1. Cut the tops off of 2 large red bell peppers and remove the stem.
2. For each pepper, make a cut straight down the side of the pepper, remove the seeds and white pith of the stem and ribs. Make another vertical cut to create 2 halves.
3. Generously brush a baking sheet with olive oil and place the pepper halves on it, skin side up, in a single layer. Brush with olive oil and cover the sheet with aluminum foil.
4. Bake in preheated 400° F oven for 20 minutes or until tender. Remove from oven and allow to cool.
5. Peel the skin off the peppers before making pesto.

To make pesto:

1. Toast garlic cloves with their skins on in a small heavy pan over medium heat until slightly brown, about 10 minutes. Transfer to a plate, cool, and peel.
2. Put garlic, roasted red peppers, parsley, cheese, and salt in a food processor and process until finely minced.
3. With processor on, slowly pour oil through food chute; process until well blended.
4. Spoon into small container and store in the refrigerator. Or freeze portions up to 1 month.

Makes about ¾ cup

Simply Elegant and Easy Pesto

Roasted Red Pepper Pizza Wedges

1 6-inch pita bread
1 tablespoon extra-virgin olive oil
2 tablespoons Roasted Red Pepper Pesto
2 tablespoons shredded mozzarella cheese

Preheat oven to 425° F.

1. Drizzle oil on top of bread.
2. Spread pesto over top of bread.
3. Sprinkle top with cheese.
4. Bake pizza at 425° F for 5 minutes or until crisp and warmed through.
5. Cut into 6 wedges and serve.

Serves 1 (6 wedges)

Pepperoncini Pesto

Superb sandwich spread to add zest to your deli cold cuts!

2 large cloves garlic
1 cup canned pepperoncini, stems pulled out (removing seed core) or cut off,
½ cup lightly packed fresh parsley leaves, stems removed
¼ cup grated Parmesan or Romano cheese
⅛ teaspoon salt
¼ cup extra-virgin olive oil

1. Place pepperoncini, parsley, garlic, cheese, and salt in a food processor and process until finely minced.
2. With processor on, slowly pour oil through food chute; process until well blended.
3. Spoon into small container and store in the refrigerator. Or freeze portion up to 1 month.

Makes about ¾ cup

Roast Beef and Pepperoncini Pesto Sandwiches

16 slices deli roast beef
1 French bread (herbed) baguette, 16- to 20-inches long, cut into 5- to 6-inch lengths or 4 5- to 6-inch long French rolls, split horizontally
¾ cup Pepperoncini Pesto
2 cups shredded Romaine lettuce
1 thinly sliced tomato

Preheat oven to 400° F.

1. Arrange the bread slices on a heavy large baking sheet, cut sides up. Bake until heated, about 2 to 3 minutes.
2. Arrange bread on work surface. Spread the top and bottom half with 1½ tablespoons (divided between the two bread halves) of pesto. Sprinkle with shredded Romaine lettuce and a few slices of the sliced tomato (be sure to evenly divide the lettuce and tomato into fourths). Top each with 4 slices of roast beef.
3. Cut sandwiches in half on diagonal, if desired. Transfer sandwiches to plates and serve.

Serves 4

About the Author

Mary El-Baz, Ph.D. is the author of five books on nutrition and fitness, including the popular titles *Easy and Healthful Mediterranean Cooking; Flavoring with Culinary Herbs: Tips, Recipes, and Cultivation;* and *The Essence of Herbal and Floral Teas.*

Made in the USA